The Shadow of Death

poems by

Jodi Andrews

Finishing Line Press
Georgetown, Kentucky

The Shadow of Death

For my love, Joel and my rocks, my parents

Copyright © 2018 by Jodi Andrews
ISBN 978-1-63534-761-6 First Edition
All rights reserved under International and Pan-American Copyright Conventions.
No part of this book may be reproduced in any manner whatsoever without written permission from the publisher, except in the case of brief quotations embodied in critical articles and reviews.

ACKNOWLEDGMENTS

1001 Journal "My Open Abdomen"
Anomaly Journal "New Life" & "My Fish Transfers Tanks"
Dark Matter Journal "Harvest"
Pasque Petals "And Slip"
The Remembered Arts Journal "Wouldn't You?"
Touch: A Journal of Healing "Gold"

Publisher: Leah Maines

Editor: Christen Kincaid

Cover Art: TJ Moore using artwork purchased from Shutterstock:
  Goldfish fly on balloon by Sergey Nivens and
  a fish bowl, isolated on white by Rose Carson
Typeface: Katie Nielson

Author Photo: Angela Boersma, Rae Studios

Printed in the USA on acid-free paper.
Order online: www.finishinglinepress.com
    also available on amazon.com

Author inquiries and mail orders:
Finishing Line Press
P. O. Box 1626
Georgetown, Kentucky 40324
U. S. A.

Table of Contents

Cancer Center 1

And Slip 2

The Disease 3

Harvest 4

Gold 5

Good News 6

While I Slept 7

My Open Abdomen 8

New Life 9

As If 10

Pain 11

Just a Poke 12

I Have 13

I Sidestepped the Valley 14

Fear, ... 15

The Scan 16

Preservation 17

My Fish Transfers Tanks 18

Wouldn't you? 19

Hope 20

Cancer Center

Flowers painted by broad brush
strokes, reds and purples framed,
evenly spaced down wide hallways.
All the places we'd rather be.

Hot air balloons static. Finches
silent, yellow. In the waiting room,
I sign my wristband. The receptionist
unpeels the scanner, sticks it to me.

Glass displays of wigged mannequin
heads sit silently around corners. A sign—
above the bathroom sink *1 in 8 women*
will get breast cancer at some point in her life.

We hear someone's buzzer beeping,
like at Olive Garden. I finger mine, feel
its smooth Sticker *19*. Hope it will buzz soon.
Hope it never does. I picture myself running

into the paintings we passed, pushing aside
endless flowers, laying in an open field,
fleeing the oncologist's "suspicious nodes,"
especially what ifs, especially death.

And Slip

slowly time moves
i cannot feel it touch
my skin, my stomach
i bend over it as if a bridge
covering rushing waters
in their cars, coffee shops,
offices they swim among
droplets below

jealous
of the flow   cancer in
my lymph nodes

leaves flutter in wind, clouds float
and I hang on to monkey bars—
the ground miles and miles
and miles below, my legs
dangle, fingers sweat and slip

The Disease

Door open, the surgeon's
about to leave the room
when she says, in an effort
to be encouraging, "We're all
very interested in the disease."
It would please her to diagnose
me so they could study my lymph
nodes, my rebellious cells under
microscopes, discuss them at
conferences—my chart open
on her desk. Coffee mug in her
right hand, she sips peacefully—
the disease only in her head.

Harvest

My medical report
read: *A chain of mesenteric*

lymph nodes was harvested
off of the vascular supply

of the terminal ileum.
Demeter, goddess of the harvest,

and life cycles—the wheel of life
and death, ever crushing—

my lymph nodes are ripe for plucking.
The OED reads harvest: season's

yield of any natural product.
Mine unnatural. Mine white on the PET scan.

In February before the Earth greens,
globes of enlarged lymph nodes ripen.

Gold

Small scale mining
to extract gold from below
sand and rock and water.
Small environmental impact.
My body—maybe gold inside,
maybe coal, maybe death.
The radiologist pokes a thick needle,
seven samples to test cells.

Seven samples to test cells,
the radiologist pokes a thick needle.
Maybe coal, maybe death
maybe gold inside my body.
Small environmental impact.
Sand and rock and water
to extract gold from below.
Small scale mining.

Good News

You don't have cancer he smiles
while I wake up from surgery
eyelids drooping. While

medicine drips liquid streams,
a bandage spans my lower abdomen;
I'm too afraid to peek at a centipede

of stitches. I expect to celebrate. Instead,
I record pain meds: ibuprophen,
oxycodone, stool softener. I thread

days together with sleep, food, exercise. When
I shower, water trickles over new, pink skin,
erodes my ability to avoid the scar again.

I long for the joy of bending down, tying,
my own shoes, sleeping on my stomach
I complain, ache & ache —how soon

I forget the strength it took to lean
on a brown covered table with wheels,
and walk around the nurse's desk cleaning

the floor with textured socks and tears
into the rest of my years.

While I Slept

He explained the procedure I would undergo while I slept.
He would try laparoscopy through my bellybutton while I slept.

When I awoke, I felt the bandage span across my abs.
I knew he'd sliced the space between fingers—bloody inches— while I slept.

The night before surgery I scrubbed my stomach to sterilize with pink
soap, memorized my smooth, peach-fuzzed skin before I slept.

Women used to go in for a biopsy and awake without a breast,
dread, fear what may disappear, happen while they slept.

If he needed to, he would cut a line—he spaced the air between
his thumb and forefinger, inches apart—he'd make the decision while I slept.

Awake, I study the pink scar, provide it with lotion,
vitamin E. I still feel its dense scar tissue bend while I sleep.

My Open Abdomen

A red rose blossomed

No black nodes
Skin peeled—petals

Stitches, suchors
Thorny stem

Pink skin buds
Among black scabs

New Life

Pregnant with a scar- tissue baby—vertical
incision from my belly button down.

My friend's belly expands. Little feet
and hands move across her globe.

Scans show the outline of limbs, head,
mouth, nose and genitals. My scan shows

suspicious lymph nodes. The OB/GYN
cuts through layers of skin and abs and

eases baby and placenta out. My friend's
awake, can hear the cry. I'm under general

anesthesia. The surgeon plucks out lymph
nodes—stacked—ballooned.

She has a new life to show for the scabby
line of scar and so do I. She absorbs each

facial expression, each yawn, squirm. People
travel miles to coo, to hold, to adore.

My proof of new life beneath shirts. Alone,
I study its details and wait for one of us to blink.

As If

The surgeon's words—weeks earlier
echo: *If this is melanoma, it's stage four.*
Some patients react quite well to medication,
but patients with melanoma like this die from it.

I sat up on the exam table. The surgeon.
His resident and nurse. My parents. Alone
in the desert. My tears the only sign of life
for miles. My body abandoning me.

Driving on the edge of the Grand Canyon,
my tire slips. Weeks later, I return
to my rhythm grading papers at the library,
eating fruit snacks, a bag of chips,

watching presidential debates to pass the time.
I throw out flowers friends gifted after surgery—
moldy stems and browned daisies.
I wonder how I can just go on as if

I was never afraid to die. As if the scar
on my belly means annoying recovery
and not holy shit they could have found
cancer. As if others don't hear they do

have cancer. As if it's all arbitrary and I
can watch comedies my life away and be
happy. As if I had no regrets. As if I have
dragon scales for skin.

Pain

My body and I are fighting again—
pain screams at me, strident. Blood
drips from my ears. Pain pounds its fists
against blood vessels, skin. It kicks
my organs to a pulp, wakes me
like a hungry baby in the middle
of the night. Refuses food, still cries.
I offer it a warm bath, but it pulls arrows
back on bows. The endless twang
and bulls eye. I offer an apple, water,
salmon. It throbs—red, explodes
firecrackers. I offer medicine, a short walk.
It cackles at my pleads for health,
my bargaining. I attempt to walk
around it, dismiss it, but it cuts, whips,
slices, severs, kills and no one else
can
hear
a
sound.

Just a Poke

she promises. I shake my wrists
to prepare, breathe in and out, squirm.
She says *You're like a man—*
the women usually can handle
a poke. I pull my wrist away, strangle
the chair arms. She says, *You better*
not plan on having children.
She wields a needle, wears scrubs.
Maybe your husband should carry
the kids for you. I don't laugh.
She squeezes my middle finger
for three drops of blood on cotton balls.
Pulls the inside outside like lymph nodes
a few months ago. But she's right.
I know nothing of pain.

I Have

I have sat naked
under hospital paper clothes
hours. Waiting for the knife.

Slept through the night
before, knowing pain will
follow, an IV drip will flow,

and I will need help standing, going pee.
I have smiled on the operating table
immunotherapy possibly ahead.

"We're like a pit crew," the nurse joked,
stuck electrodes, inserted fluids.
I have roared before the plunge into sleep.

I have boasted courage when my parents,
husband offered to take my place. I have
endured the pain, neglected more meds,

swung back up on the saddle, latched my
seatbelt over a wounded abdomen,
and snarled at death—not yet.

I sidestepped the valley

of the shadow of death.
The surgeon etched a straight line
between the unknown and known.
He mapped my path to life,
drew the river line. On the cliff,
my eyes refocused.
How far down is that?
I walked a narrow path—
the right
a steep climb,
the left
a steep fall.
Dizzy steps across the ledge.
The gift of slipping rocks,
canyon echoes then solid ground;
too easy to forget how fragile
until my jeans button too tight,
my shirt slips up and proof, pink
and smooth against white skin—
Alive! Alive! Alive, I am!

Fear,

You twist my stomach into
a noose, shoot arrows
from my hips when a needle
pulls blood, knot muscles near
my shoulder blade and twist
them tight around your knife.
Thistles tangle through my body,
too deep, too sharp to extract
these swaths of shadows. My doctor
says stress is associated with all
of its own diseases: certain cancers,
heart disease, and others. If
the pathology results don't kill
me, all your twisting just might.

The Scan

Back under the white scanner's arm
I remember last year's radiation
leaking through skin, the phone call:

suspicious lymph nodes referred
to Mayo Clinic: and on the report—
the patient was emotional.

This week my habit of peeling
skin off my fingers worsened.
I pulled too far, exposed pink

layers beneath finger after finger.
To soothe, I put them in my mouth
like thread before the needle's eye.

It will scan me in "slices," expose
secrets my body hides. The machine
pulls my body back and says "breathe."

I am thankful for the reminder—
my arms stretched above my head,
wrists touching, a hostage awaiting fate.

Preservation

A soft breeze sways leafy trees,
hairs that have come loose from
my French braid. The air hums again.
Orange construction cones bloom
like Echinacea. Amaryllis petals
unfurl, curl their lips outward and sing.
Elm leaves sprout and spread jagged
edges toward the sun. It's been a year,
and in warm sunlight, I forget how fear feels,
having shivered in chilly winds, snapped
at the stalk, dropped like all the leaves.
Until then, I'll open in vibrant yellows,
pinks, purples, I'll bloom. I'll wave life
high into the heavens. I'll duct tape
the leaves to myself if I have to.

My Fish Transfers Tanks

I reach blue handled mesh
into disappearing water.
My burgundy beta eyes it
and drifts
to the opposite side
of the bowl.
I move netting closer. He swims
the other way.
I think of the follow-up ultrasound
scheduled a week from today.
A cyst on my ovary. The scar near
there ached earlier in the cereal aisle.
I wish I could swim forever away
from this body's downfalls,
but I can feel the mesh moving
closer. It chases me around
in circles until it snatches me,
and I am exposed: jerking,
breathless and afraid.

Wouldn't You?

If you think you might be dying and then
you aren't, wouldn't you sing birds into
windows to help you fold sheets,
and tie bows into flowy, satin dresses?
Wouldn't you sweep the floor with joy, lug
laundry up three flights of stairs to a machine
that half works with a smile on your face?
Wouldn't you scrub dishes to the beat
of your favorite song? Pay your bills
while dancing? Your heart beating, skin feeling.
Wouldn't you run outside till you're out of breath?
Stay up late and watch the stars just to feel tiny?

Instead, I crawled into myself
like a turtle scared for its soft body.

Just the other day I felt light again— laughing
till I couldn't breathe, tickling my husband while
he tickled back. I trusted my body. Tumbled
back handsprings on a four-inch beam.
Landed. Arms in the air, smiling.

Hope

Now, as scans and tests
read healthy, babies, a house
with a screened in porch,
growing old ahead again,
so I blow hope into purple
balloons at the survivor's
march, lasso the ribbons
to my wrist, hundreds, and float.

Jodi Andrews was born and raised in eastern South Dakota. She loves the wide-open skies and the small-town life that Brookings has to offer. She teaches English classes at South Dakota State University, including composition and technical communication. When she was student teaching and about to graduate with her BA, she was diagnosed with a melanoma on the side of her right knee. Two years later, she had surgery to extract enlarged lymph nodes from her abdomen to test them for melanoma because the oncologist thought the original cancer had spread.

In her debut chapbook of poetry, *The Shadow of Death*, she explores these experiences, and practices what one of her college professors, Dr. Charles Woodard, encouraged his students to do: turn negative experience into positive energy.

Andrews has been seriously writing poetry since the Fall of 2015, when she finally took a poetry class in graduate school. She has had poems published in several journals including *Anomaly Literary Journal*, *Dark Matter Journal*, *The Remembered Arts Journal*, *Unlost Journal*, *Calamus Journal*, and others. She also serves on the board of directors for the South Dakota State Poetry Society as the blog/website manager and the annual contest manager.

www.ingramcontent.com/pod-product-compliance
Lightning Source LLC
LaVergne TN
LVHW041525070426
835507LV00013B/1838